D1274399

The Conference Board

Restructuring Education

educators, public/private-sector authorities focus on:

- *changing needs of employers*
- *changing composition of student bodies*
- *overcoming inertia in the system*
- *business-education partnerships*

Research Report No. 902

ABOUT THE CONFERENCE BOARD

The Conference Board is a business information service whose purpose is to assist senior executives and other leaders in arriving at sound decisions. Since its founding in 1916, the Board has been creating close personal networks of leaders who exchange experience and judgment on significant issues in management practice, economics and public policy. The networks are supported by an international program of research and meetings which The Conference Board staff of more than 350 persons carries out from offices in New York, Ottawa and Brussels.

More than 3,600 organizations in over 50 nations participate in The Conference Board's work as Associates. The Board is a not-for-profit corporation and the greatest share of its financial support comes from business concerns, many with worldwide operations. The Board also has many Associates among labor unions, colleges and universities, government agencies, libraries and trade and professional associations.

The Conference Board, Inc.
845 Third Avenue
New York, New York 10022
(212) 759-0900
RCA International Telex
237282 and 234465

The Conference Board, Inc.
Avenue Louise, 207 - Bte 5
B-1050 Brussels, Belgium
(02) 640 62 40
Telex: 63635

The Conference Board, Inc.
1755 Massachusetts Avenue, N.W.
Suite 312
Washington, D.C. 20036
(202) 483-0580

The Conference Board of Canada
255 Smyth Road
Ottawa, Ontario K1H 8M7
(613) 526-3280

Conference Board Research Report No. 902   Printed in U.S.A.

© 1987 THE CONFERENCE BOARD, INC.

ISBN NO.:0-8237-0345-2

Restructuring Education
Highlights of a Conference

Edited by Melissa A. Berman

A Report from The Conference Board

OLIN LIBRARY ROLLINS COLLEGE

LC
466
.R47
1987

Contents

Why This Report

Leaders from all sectors of U.S. society are virtually unanimous in their agreement that education is of vital importance to the enterprise system and to our way of life. Concern about industrial competitiveness has added fresh urgency to efforts to improve the learning process through business-education partnerships.

The distinguished speakers from The Conference Board's 1987 meeting on business and education addressed key questions of this issue: not just what should be changed, but how this change should be managed. Their insights and analyses offer valuable perspectives to executives involved in reshaping policy and designing company partnership programs. The Conference Board is grateful to these speakers for their thoughtful contributions.

JAMES T. MILLS
President

Introduction

The Conference Board's 1987 meeting "A New Education Agenda for Business," held in Washington, D.C., drew national attention from leaders in education, public policy, business and from the media. This volume presents the highlights of that conference, including formal addresses and workshop discussions. The conference was planned and directed by Leonard Lund, Senior Research Associate at The Conference Board.

Educational issues captured the attention of many businesses in 1983, with the release of *A Nation At Risk,* the report of the National Commission on Excellence in Education, which focused national attention on educational reform and set the terms of the debate. Research conducted by organizations like The Conference Board, the Carnegie Foundation, and the Committee for Economic Development helped move the business community's role into the forefront of initiatives.

In the last year or two, as many speakers noted, educational reform has entered a "second wave" in which experts and observers agreed that "more and better" (as in more class time and higher standards for both teachers and students) were not enough: The educational system needs to be different—and in fundamental ways. More recently, educational reform itself has come in for critical attention. Some school-jobs programs have been labeled failures; a new study questions the impact of recent efforts to improve student performance.[1] Meaningful reform, many insist, must consider the changing requirements of the U.S. job market.

With this broadened perspective, the speakers and participants at The Conference Board's 1987 meeting concentrated on identifying effective ways for business to participate in changing the fundamentals of the educational system, at the local and policy levels. The business community, many concluded, should explain more thoroughly what kinds of skills its work force will need; should provide guidance and expertise on management and appraisal of the school system; and should involve top management in the planning process. Partnerships can thus grapple with the problems of defining and teaching the sophisticated skills required on the job now and with the difficulties confronting children "at risk."

[1]*Educational Achievements: Explanations and Implications of Recent Trends.* Congressional Budget Office, Washington, D.C., August, 1987.

The consensus of the views and ideas offered at the conference were summarized by Professor Peter Dobkin Hall of Yale University, an education historian who attended the meeting:

> If business seriously intends to shape the education agenda in the United States, it must set its sights more broadly. It must fully accept the fact that the business corporation is an instrument of social change—whether or not it is willing to exercise its power for change. The major waves of American education reform originated in and were carried forward by socially concerned business communities that freely acknowledged the ties between private profit and the public good.

MELISSA A. BERMAN

Who's Who in This Report

Bill Clinton, *Governor of Arkansas*

Governor Clinton has been instrumental in developing state policy in the areas of education, economic development, and criminal justice. In 1983 Governor Clinton called the Arkansas Legislature into special session to enact new standards for public schools and an increase in the sales tax to support these improvements in higher and vocational education. Governor Clinton has served as Chairman of the National Governors' Association and Chairman of the Education Commission of the States. In a 1986 Newsweek magazine poll, he was selected by his fellow governors as one of the five most effective governors in the nation.

Badi G. Foster, *President, AEtna Institute for Corporate Education*

Dr. Foster has been in his present position since 1981. He is responsible for corporate education programs ranging from human resources to data-processing training. He also oversees the Institute's management consulting activities, educational technology and research, and AEtna's educational involvement with outside organizations. Dr. Foster came to AEtna from Harvard University where his positions included Director of Field Experience Program, Graduate School of Education, and Assistant Director, Kennedy Institute.

Edward A. Fox, *President and Chief Executive Officer, Student Loan Marketing Association (Sallie Mae)*

Mr. Fox was appointed to his present position in April of 1973. Prior to joining Sallie Mae, he served as Chief Financial Officer and Administrator of the Federal Home Loan Bank System. Mr. Fox previously held a variety of corporate finance and investment management positions with Procter & Gamble, Studebaker-Worthington Corporation, and the Mobile Oil Corporation. He is a Member of the Advisory Board of the National Center on Financial Services and was appointed by President Reagan to the Fisk University Board of Advisors.

Ted Kolderie, *Senior Fellow, Hubert H. Humphrey Institute of Public Affairs, University of Minnesota*

Mr. Kolderie has been in his present position since 1980. Prior to that he was reporter and editorial writer for the *Minnesota Star and Tribune* and editor of "The Bottom Line," a weekly radio public affairs program in the Twin Cities area. He was Executive Director of the Citizens League from 1967 to 1980 and still serves as a member of the League's Board of Directors.

Marsha Levine, *Associate Director, Education Issues, American Federation of Teachers*

Dr. Levine is co-director of a major study of business and the public schools published by the Committee for Economic Development. As a Visiting Fellow in Education Policy Studies at the American Enterprise Institute, she studied the potential for expanded relationships between corporations and public schools. Dr. Levine taught for eight years in public and private schools at the primary and secondary levels. She developed and directed Professional Development Centers for teacher education and staff development at the University of Maryland.

Patrick R. Manders, *Publisher/General Manager, ProEducation Publications*

Mr. Manders has been in his present position since March of 1984. Since 1981 he has also served as Director of Communications of Modern Talking Picture Service, the parent company of ProEducation.

Donald M. Stewart, *President, The College Board*

Mr. Stewart took office as President of the College Board on January 1st, 1987. He was previously the sixth President of Spelman College. From 1970 to 1976 he was at the University of Pennsylvania as Executive Assistant to the President, instructor in city planning and public policy analysis, and Associate Dean of Arts and Sciences. Mr. Stewart is a trustee of the Committee for Economic Development and the President's Committee on the Arts and Humanities. He is a member of the Council on Foreign Relations and the National Advisory Committee on Accreditation and Institutional Eligibility of the U.S. Department of Education.

Workshop Leaders

Workshop 1

Rita G. Kaplan, *former Corporate Manager, Education Programs, Honeywell, Inc.*

Guiding the company's strategies for elementary and secondary education, Ms. Kaplan worked with the Minneapolis schools in the design of the Summatech magnet program and founded Education Ventures, Inc., a nonprofit corporation providing incentives for excellence in teaching and learning. Ms. Kaplan continues to consult on issues related to education as well as on human resources and strategic programs related to social policy.

Anthony Carnevale, *Vice President and Chief Economist, American Society for Training and Development (ASTD)*

Prior to joining ASTD, Dr. Carnevale served as Director of Government Relations for the American Federation of State, County, and Municipal Employees of the AFL-CIO. From 1975 to 1978, he was a Senior Budget, Appropriations and Authorization Analyst for the Senate Committee on the Budget. He was a Senior Policy Analyst in the Department of Health, Education, and Welfare from 1973 to 1975.

Workshop 2

Jo Ann Swinney, *Director of Community Affairs, Tenneco, Inc.*

Ms. Swinney is responsible for corporate contributions, federated campaigns, and all employee-related community involvement programs for Tenneco. She initiated Tenneco's Volunteers In Assistance (VIA), Jefferson Davis/Tenneco Business School Partnership, and a Summer Jobs Youth Employment Training Program that received President Reagan's Private Sector Initiatives Award. VIA also received President Reagan's Volunteer Action Award and the Governor's Corporate Volunteer Award.

Gordon B. Bonfield, *Senior Vice President and Group Executive, Tenneco, Inc.*

Since reaching his present position in 1982, Mr. Bonfield has had overall responsibility for corporate affairs, state governmental affairs, and industrial ecology. He previously was Chairman of Packaging Corporation of America. Mr. Bonfield serves as a Senior Fellow of the American Leadership Forum, as Chairman of the Houston Job Training Partnership Council, as President and board member of the Texas Institute for Arts in Education, and as a board member for the State Advisory Council of the Job Training Partnership Act.

Workshop 3

Renee A. Berger, *President, Teamworks, Inc.*

Ms. Berger has 15 years of consulting experience in the fields of management training, project design and evaluation, and research and reporting. Before establishing Teamworks, she served as the Director of Partnerships for the White House Task Force on Private Sector Initiatives. She has been a consultant for numerous organizations in the United States and abroad, including The Conference Board, German Marshall Fund, Organization for Economic Cooperation and Development (Paris), and the Committee for Economic Development. Ms. Berger is the author of several books and articles.

Sue E. Berryman, *Director, Institute on Education and the Economy and Director, National Center on Education and Employment, Teachers College, Columbia University*

Dr. Berryman has been in her present position since 1986. Prior to joining the Institute she was with The Rand Corporation as Behavioral Scientist, Behavioral Sciences Department and Resident Consultant, Washington Research Division. Dr. Berryman has worked with organizations such as the Graduate Management Admission Council, National Commission for Employment Policy, the Rockefeller Foundation, the Ford Foundation, and the Departments of Labor and Education.

Workshop 4

Daniel F. Morley, *Vice President and Director, Public Affairs, State Street Bank and Trust Company*

Mr. Morley was a founder and President of the Boston Private Industry Council, Inc., a public-private venture bringing innovative approaches to the areas of school-to-work transition and educational reform. He is the President of Goals for Boston and is past President of the Boston Housing Partnership, Inc. Mr. Morley is also Chairman of the State Street Foundation. He is an advisor to the Massachusetts Business Roundtable, the Center for Business and Government of the Kennedy School of Government of Harvard University, The Conference Board's Community and Public Issues Council, and the Council of Foundations' Committee on Corporate Philanthropy.

Sol Hurwitz, *Senior Vice President, Committee for Economic Development (CED)*

Mr. Hurwitz joined CED in 1966 as Associate Director of Information and a year later became Director of Information. He was named Vice President in 1972 and Senior Vice President in 1980. He has taught at the New School for Social Research and is presently a member of the Board of Trustees of the Joint Council on Economic Education and the Boards of Directors of Public/Private Ventures and the Public Education Fund.

The Common Agenda: Liberating Undreamed-Of Talent

The Honorable Bill Clinton
Governor of Arkansas
Chairman, Education Commission
of the United States

More than two centuries ago, Thomas Jefferson argued that vast potential for genius and leadership lay untapped throughout the world. He called for a more general diffusion of knowledge across Virginia and the other colonies in order to create "an aristocracy of virtue and talent" that would lead the country through its great experiment with democracy. For Jefferson, education was the key to two kinds of liberation: the liberation of men from despotic rulers and institutions; and the liberation of energies and imagination from within the "common man."

Then, education was necessary to create an America of our founders' vision. Now, education is necessary to sustain the country that emerged from that vision, an America capable of providing opportunity at home and of prompting peace and prosperity around the world. Whether we can meet that challenge is open to question.

Confronting New Challenges

Formidable internal and external challenges to our prosperity and position in the world force upon all of us a common agenda, a distinctively American agenda: to unleash the underdeveloped, even undreamed-of talents of our people. But the business, educational and governmental institutions sufficient to the needs of earlier times are no longer sufficient to the challenges of the 21st century.

Let me frame the challenges from the point of view of a governor whose state feels keenly the burden of our competitive difficulties—lost farms, idle factory workers, and aching poor. Low-wage workers with very basic skills and minimal competence are available in many parts of the world. They are highly motivated and eager to work for wages Americans cannot live on. If comparative labor costs are the determining factor in our competitive position, we are bound to fail. On that score, the Japanese are already finding themselves in a similar position with respect to Korea, Taiwan, and other newly-industrialized nations of the Pacific Basin, even in some high-tech areas.

This nation must either work toward some sort of high-wage, high-technology, innovative economy—or ask each succeeding generation to accept a lower standard of living. This process, in fact, began in 1973, when real median income started to decline. Although 9.3 million new jobs were created between 1979 and 1985, 44 percent were at or below the poverty level, twice the percentage of poverty jobs created in the previous six-year period. Between 1981 and 1986, four out of ten Americans experienced a decline in real income. This drift cannot be allowed to continue. The only way to stop it is by increasing the efficiency by which we do old things, or by finding new things to do that are not yet subject to undercutting by overseas competitors.

If business is going to create jobs that are more appropriate, the people must be there to fill them. In spite of the progress attained since the issuance of *A Nation At Risk* (The National Commission on Excellence in Education, *A Nation at Risk: The Imperative for Educational Reform.* April, 1983.) we are a long way from where we need to be. A Public Opinion Laboratory study found most Americans "scientifically illiterate"—only minimally conversant with basic scientific facts, ideas and processes. Recent comparisons of American students' achievement in mathematics to that of students in other countries are equally dismaying. Clearly, schools will need to enable a much larger segment of the population to acquire a comprehensive understanding of science, mathematics and technology. Even those citizens who have no interest in being technical workers will have to understand complex technical and scientific issues to make responsible public policy and the kinds of judgments our democracy requires of its citizens.

A high-technology, high-wage economy calls for more than improved achievement in science and mathematics. It calls for much higher levels of general literacy; more widespread sophistication in reasoning, analyzing, and interpreting information. An advanced economy will demand more creativity, more mental flexibility, and more capacity to adapt to rapidly changing work requirements and job structures.

Problems in Schools

Unfortunately, there have been steady declines in the proportion of students demonstrating higher literacy skills, such as analytical writing, problem solving, critical thinking, argument, analysis, synthesis, interpretation and evaluation. Most recent reports from the National Assessment of Educational Progress make it clear that although most U.S. students easily meet the lower literacy standards of a generation ago, a majority do not meet today's higher standards and are unlikely to meet tomorrow's.

Researchers paint a gloomy picture of most schools' capacity to turn the trend around. In his comprehensive work on schooling, John Goodlad has found that very few classrooms are conducive to training in and practice of higher-order thinking skills. Teachers monopolize classroom discussion, out-talking entire classrooms of students by a large ratio. Extended discussion, writing and rewriting, debate, and all other ways in which students develop more sophisticated information-processing skills are simply not present in many classrooms. And Goodlad found that even teachers who want to cultivate such skills in their students either do not know how or find themselves constrained by the structural conditions of teaching and schooling.

Paramount among those conditions is the need to control large numbers of restless students in a small space. Other conditions conspire with this management problem to make it difficult for teachers to try innovative programs, spend more than a few minutes on any task, attend to individual needs that require writing, or reduce their dependence on the lecture. Many noneducational duties absorb time desperately needed by teachers for planning complex learning activities and for collaborating with colleagues about how the school should be run to achieve its mission. A grasp of how different subjects relate to one another—how mathematics relates to science, for instance, or how both relate to history—is out of the question.

Most troubling, this study finds that to the extent that training in higher thinking skills appeared anywhere, it appeared in the courses reserved for the college-bound student. Students in general education, vocational education, or in low-track courses were being instructed in very fundamentally defined basics. These students, disproportionately minorities and disadvantaged children, at risk in many social and educational ways, are subjected to the drill, practice and rote methods of learning that do not lead to creativity or to any capacity to interpret, analyze, synthesize or solve problems. They are being trained with an industrial model of literacy that will not serve them well in the years ahead, in schools that are organized along rigid, hierarchical, old-fashioned lines.

The already limited capacity of many schools to respond to the challenge from without is strained further by the internal threat to their success. Increasing numbers of elementary and secondary students come from racial minorities and poor single-parent households. Many come from homes in which English is not the dominant language. High proportions of young people are growing up in conditions that weaken their motivation, their capacity to learn, their concern for others and their belief in the future.

Like the international challenge, this national challenge is one we can not shirk. Schools are simply going to have to do a much better job of educating students. Instead of weeding them out or doing them in with watered-down courses, schools will have to find new ways to develop latent talents. Not to address this problem is to acquiesce to the crippling of a large proportion of young people, to drift toward a two-tiered society that has been developing more rapidly in the past five years, and to invite a continued increase in the gap between rich and poor.

The Second Wave of Reform: Restructuring

In its hour of need, education requires help from the corporate community more than ever before. During the so-called "first wave" of educational reform, from about the time of *A Nation At Risk* to the present, business people supported massive efforts to stem educational decline. They helped to sell the need for more rigorous courses, smaller classes, more attention to the basics, more revenue to pay for the reform.

To meet the challenge before us, education must go through a second wave of reform which goes to the heart of the learning process—focusing on how schools are run, how teachers teach, what students do, and what the state requires in the way of regulations or paperwork. To capture the essence of what needs to be done, education has borrowed a "buzz word" from corporate America: restructuring.

In education (as in business) restructuring may take on different meanings from school to school, but everywhere it means vastly improving productivity so that more students stay in school and are exposed to much more of what they need to know. It means changing the system of instruction, making better use of time, creating an atmosphere more conducive to learning, and integrating technology more efficiently. It means leading schools more effectively with shared decision making at the school level, less bureaucracy, and more effective alliances with health, welfare and juvenile justice programs.

Some schools may have to be restructured in order to retrain unemployed workers and to accommodate changing work situations within families. Schools might conceivably be open all day, into the evening, all year, to accommodate diverse community needs. Restructuring in many cases will mean decentralizing districts stifled by their own bureaucracy and flattening management structures. Extremely large schools might be broken up into schools-within-schools.

Teachers can be empowered with a far greater say in the running of the school, something other professionals traditionally have enjoyed and which more and more factory workers have begun to enjoy, here and abroad. Teachers' work itself can be restructured with creative uses of technology. The teachers' role as a repository of facts is doomed by information technology. New definitions of teaching will inevitably emerge. Classrooms need not have four walls and 35 seats lined up in rows. They can be anywhere as long as learning is taking place.

Restructuring Policy

State policy needs restructuring as well. For decades, policymakers have focused their attention on minimum standards. That is their duty: to assure the public that its tax-supported institutions are functioning fairly and efficiently.

But there are limits to what we can accomplish with policies oriented toward the minimum, and their effect on teachers and administrators may sometimes be to prevent excellence as well as to mandate minimum performance. If state policy for funding programs and certifying teachers discourages innovation, we will not get the experimentation we so desperately need. State leaders have to find policy tools that inspire, rather than deaden, educators; that forge links, rather than create educational fiefdoms; that empower people, rather than enslave them to bureaucratic routine and paperwork.

There are, of course, many obstacles to these kinds of change. State agency and local administrative control is deeply entrenched and there is great, often justified, fear that too much deregulation could lead to falling minimums rather than rising maximums. The system of selecting, training, evaluating and rewarding school leaders seldom encourages both competition and innovation. Entrenched bureaucracies—from teacher colleges to administrator groups to teacher unions—often fight harder for their turf and their retirement benefits than for more flexible, open and efficient ways of educating children. A powerful inertia grips the system. Many within it have tired of state mandates piled on the already considerable burden of their jobs and have decided to "wait this one out," as they have waited out reforms in the past.

Leadership Inside and Outside the System

You can try to change a complex system like this through outside pressure and influence, but without the support of people inside the system not much will happen. On the other hand, people inside the system will never change it radically without the help of policymakers, community leaders, business leaders, and others outside the system. The key to success in the next stage of reform is to get people inside and outside the system to work in tandem.

If we are going to tap the vast untapped potential of our students, it is going to require new kinds of leadership up and down the line. The leadership we need recognizes the permanence of the change and the primary importance of people over all other resources. It recognizes the necessity of reaching out to build communities of purpose within the schools, with business, and with other allies beyond the schools. It sees the imperative to restructure schools (as many businesses were) in order to place responsibility for solving problems where it belongs, with the people closest to those problems.

We can develop this kind of leadership and learning in our schools only if good business people are prepared to make personal commitments of time and energy. I am optimistic about this because it is clear that more and more private-sector leaders recognize that we cannot rebuild America solely with the heroic triumphs of individual entrepreneurs, as important as they are.

There is much the business community can do to help. Many state and local school leaders are willing to restructure education by eliminating management layers and reducing regulations, if they can do it without reducing quality—but they don't know how. Business leaders' involvement with children at risk can dramatically change their attitudes about staying in school and learning there.

Every school district wants to increase the use of computers and other advanced technology, but money will not be spent in the most efficient manner without private-sector involvement. In Arkansas, for instance, corporate leaders started with $250,000 in private seed money which led to an increase in the percentage of our schools with computers from 15 to 87 percent in three years.

If we want to keep the American dream alive for our own people and preserve America's role in the world, we must develop an excellent, continuously changing system for educating and training our people. To do that, we must build better partnerships between schools and businesses. We have to bring down the barriers to productivity that keep too many people out of the mainstream at a time when we need all of our people to be as productive as possible.

Education:
The Real Risks

Donald M. Stewart
President, The College Board

The report of the National Commission on Excellence in Education was much heralded when it appeared in April, 1983.[1] Are we still a "nation at risk" due to poor teaching and even poorer student performance? Has the "rising tide of mediocrity" in education at least begun to ebb? While we do not know what lasting effects the reform movement will have, the National Assessment of Educational Progress (NAEP), funded by the U.S. Department of Education, is one means of attempting to measure the nation's progress. Every five years, the National Assessment evaluates young Americans' performance in reading, mathematics and writing. From time to time, it also assesses student performance in science, social studies/citizenship, literature, music, art and career development. Each assessment is based on representative samples of nine-, thirteen- and seventeen-year-olds.

Preliminary Performance Data

The most recent NAEP reading and writing assessment was in Spring, 1984. The reading results were released in September of 1984 and the writing results in April and December of 1986. The average level of accomplishment in reading and writing had declined from 1974 to 1979; the 1984 results saw an *increase* in the average level equal to the decline between 1974 and 1979. This trend extended to all three age levels, with particularly strong gains among minorities and the poor. Despite the closing of the gap between whites and minorities, 17-year-old blacks had the reading ability of 13-year-old whites in the 1984 assessment. Improvements are evident among the basic skills, but there was an erosion of middle-range and higher-order skills.

[1]The National Commission on Excellence in Education, *A Nation at Risk: The Imperative for Educational Reform.* April, 1983.

The most recent mathematics and science assessment was Spring, 1986. The trends in math and science are similar to the 1979-84 results in reading, and consistent across the three age groups. From 1978 to 1982, gains in average scores brought the level back to that of 1974. Minority gains were twice those of whites. Improvements were observed in the basic skills; middle-range and higher-order skills deteriorated.

These data suggest that improvement in basic skills was already occurring at some time after 1979 for reading and writing and after 1978 for mathematics and science. Average scores on the Scholastic Aptitude Tests (SATs), which are reported by The College Board for millions of college-bound students each year, declined from 1963 and reached bottom in 1980. By 1982, however, the scores registered a definite upward turn. Taken together, this suggests that improvements in education were actually underway before the publication of *A Nation At Risk.*

Despite the refreshing upward tendency of recent average SAT scores (whose decline, by the way, was the first signal of a crisis in educational quality) and a few other fragmentary indicators, such as the NAEP data, we have no hard, direct evidence of real progress. Some observers point to the flurry of activity in education during the past few years, particularly within states, as evidence that progress has taken place.

State-Level Initiatives

Since 1983, between 200 and 300 state-level task forces have been at work developing reform proposals and seeking their adoption. The Education Commission of the States has catalogued 45 different kinds of reform activities that have been undertaken or proposed by various state jurisdictions. Among these activities are those involving governance, leadership, organization, finance, program design, teachers and students, parents, technology, and support services in the schools.

Within this complex framework, the two dominant themes of reform have been more rigorous academic standards for students and more recognition and higher standards for teachers. Forty-five states have changed their requirements for a standard high school diploma, almost universally in the form of increased course requirements. Six states have raised the age of release from mandatory schooling, six start pupils earlier, and three do both. Six states and the District of Columbia lengthened the school year. Some states, like California, provide incentives to individual districts to lengthen the school year or school day. Others have retained the typical five-hour day but have limited extracurricular activities, reduced interruptions, and otherwise encouraged better use of time.

Most states have reassessed their policies with respect to teachers, including certification, recognition, promotion, and compensation. Thirty-seven have created career ladders or restructured the profession. Comprehensive planning for similar reforms is under consideration in 13 states.

The pessimists note that states have slowed in their enactment of omnibus reform bills and that reforms already enacted are endangered by economic decline in states, such as Texas and Oklahoma, and by federal tax reform, which makes sales taxes less politically viable for funding education. The elimination of federally supported revenue-sharing programs has also increased pressure on the state and local tax dollar, thereby undermining state efforts to mount many educational improvement programs.

Most telling of all, critics say, is that it is "business as usual" in the overwhelming majority of U.S. classrooms. For all the rhetoric of reform, they say, fundamental changes to improve the way in which children are taught, and to make better choices about what they are taught, have not been affected. What good, they ask, is a longer school year or a longer school day, or more required courses, if it simply means more of what has already proven inadequate?

Unanswered Questions

Even if this view is, in its way, as much an overstatement as *A Nation at Risk,* it nevertheless raises important questions. Are schools intended:

- To provide a stimulating, intellectual environment?
- To compensate for other social problems or deficits?
- To provide a uniform ladder for learning—let the chips fall where they may?
- To find a way in which to maximize the capabilities of each student regardless of native intelligence or personal background?
- To prepare students for jobs?

The answers to these questions are crucial to the evaluation of whether or not we are still "a nation at risk." However, until we have a clear idea of what we want the schools to do, there is no way to say where, and if, they are failing. We also need to ask whether the results of the current reforms will be the kind that assure the future health and prosperity of American society.

Reactive Reform

Most of the rhetoric, action, and assessment of progress in the current reform movement is cast in terms of decline, of looking to a former standard of quality that has been lost and must be regained. Reformers seek to tighten and raise academic standards in order to improve academic performance by teachers and students. Thus, the U.S. approach tends to be reactive rather than proactive—in marked contrast, for example, to the efforts currently underway in Japan, where reform is aimed at liberalizing the educational system and making it less rigid.

The Japanese educational system assumes that all students can and will learn. Traditionally, sorting and selection take place at the end of junior high school and again at the point of entrance to higher education. This process is severely regulated by a series of comprehensive examinations. Serious consideration is now being given, however, to recommendations to restructure Japan's uniformly administered, comprehensive examination system and to eliminate the examination for senior high school. (These examinations are curriculum-specific and similar to the College Board's Achievement Tests.) The Japanese approach, monitored by its National Council on Educational Reform, seeks ways to enhance individuality and creativity within a uniform system that now emphasizes memorization, precision, group loyalty, and self-control.

Having caught up with the West economically and educationally, the Japanese are seemingly less concerned today about standards of academic achievement than we are. Perhaps the Japanese can now afford to relax, given their almost 100 percent literacy rate, their 95 percent retention rate through high school, and their extraordinarily high achievement rates, particularly in math and science (as measured by standardized examinations, nationally and internationally). Undoubtedly, the quality of Japan's schooling and its global economic success are directly linked. Yet, the Japanese worry about their ability to create educated workers and managers for industries and corporations in the 21st century. They also worry that they are not producing a sufficient number of Nobel laureates.

In the United States, as in Japan, corporate preferences for educated employees by type and level of achievement will have a significant impact on what students learn and how they learn as they prepare for the world of work. Narrow vocational preparation is less desirable. Mastering basic skills—reading, writing, computing, and listening—are a must. But higher-order skills of reasoning and critical thinking are necessary as well. We will be an information-based society, requiring a higher level of skills from those who hope to be employed and socially valuable. This is particularly important for minorities, given current test results.

New Demands and Opportunities Needed

The old standard worked well to socialize and train a school population headed for the labor market of an economy based on mass production. It was fully developed in its basic form and character at least a century ago; it stressed what one critic calls a "dull orderliness" of lockstep advancement, frontal teaching and passive learning, routine skills in computation and reading, and basics of democratic principles. All this was conducted within a physical setting and by a bureaucracy modeled after the factories in which most of the pupils would work.

Today, although many of those factory jobs have moved offshore, the educational reform movement is seeking to restore the schools' ability to teach those routine skills better suited to an earlier era. Employers find that high-school graduates have difficulty dealing with the increasingly complex tasks that confront them. Unfortunately, the same is being said about college graduates. Many U.S. college graduates don't learn easily on the job, can't read complicated material, have difficulty evaluating or making complex arguments, don't write well, and have difficulty using quantitative concepts and methods on unfamiliar problems. Our schools and colleges are not able to teach students how to think critically or abstractly. Like the Japanese, we must plan for the 21st century and stop looking backward.

By the end of this century, about a third of our school children will be members of minority groups, largely black and Hispanic. Present realities being what they are, that also means that many of them will be from poor backgrounds, in which the opportunity to do well academically is often missing or the value of doing well is not always self-evident. For them, new and better opportunities for motivation and success must be devised.

If our schools are unable to prepare these youngsters successfully for the demands of the new labor market, it will not merely be a matter of social injustice but an economic disaster. Our fastest-growing age and population cohort cannot continue to send proportionately fewer of its members on to higher education. And yet today's schools turn them off in droves and they drop out. As a result, they do not attend college or get good jobs. The gap between the haves and have-nots in our society, often defined in terms of race, socio-economic level and ethnic background, continues to widen at an alarming rate.

Success in rebuilding our educational system means more than teaching the different skills needed for the future. It means using new techniques to engage students with varied backgrounds and abilities, persuading them that the enterprise is worthwhile, and responding to their individual needs in ways that will enable them to succeed.

Quality of Performance

This demands a radical change in the way we think of educational accountability, and the business community has a critically important role to play here. In the old—and largely present—system, quality is typically defined in terms of standards that must be met. A successful new system will have standards that are just as high or higher, but quality will be defined in terms of the proportion of students who are enabled by the system to meet those standards. Such a definition of educational quality—performance as well as standards—can truly reconcile educational quality and equality. How can we achieve such a turnabout?

For one thing, top priority must be given to improving our teaching force. No reform will have any impact if it does not have effect in the classroom. This means rigorous reform in the training of teachers, a topic addressed by the Carnegie Foundation's report.[2] For another, we should be paying much more attention to "outcomes" than to "inputs." That is, instead of prescribing more courses or longer school years, we should define what students need to know and be able to do and then support educational practices that lead to those results.

That notion is exemplified by the College Board's Educational Equality Project. Its description of learning outcomes in six academic skill categories and six academic subjects has been adopted directly or indirectly as part of educational reform in 27 states. It also has been the stimulus for discussion and work in a great many local efforts, including 19 formal school/college partnerships across the country. Employers have enthusiastically endorsed the academic skills that the Educational Equality Project identifies as essential for new employees, thus demonstrating that academic subjects are important for all students, not just

[2]The Carnegie Forum on Education and the Economy, Task Force on Teaching as a Profession, *A Nation Prepared: Teachers for the 21st Century.* May, 1986.

the college-bound. This was the conclusion reached by the College Board's Committee for Economic Development's Business-School Task Force.

What should the role of business be in helping to create the incentive system for improved schooling? Very simply, to leave the doors of economic opportunity open for all people regardless of race, class or creed. Adopt schools and help to make them better with business know-how, but hire their graduates as well. Business has a right to demand top-flight performance from its employees, but it also has a responsibility to participate in the promotion of quality schooling. For minorities, particularly blacks and Hispanics, this means that companies must make special efforts, often falling under the much-maligned title of "affirmative action," until the educational system gets through this terribly difficult period of transition and of "catching-up." The key to our success in this effort lies in the quality of our schools.

Beyond Business-Education Partnerships

Ted Kolderie
Senior Fellow
Herbert H. Humphrey Institute of Public Affairs
University of Minnesota

Most of the discussion about improving schools centers on what the improvements ought to be: what the method of testing ought to be, how long the school day and school year ought to be, how long the teachers' training ought to be, and what the technology ought to be. But we need to think more about the critical question: How does improvement occur? Getting an idea tried is not so difficult—there are pilot projects everywhere. But too often they never get beyond the demonstration stage. The tough questions, as everybody knows, are: Do the innovations last? Do the innovations spread?

Nothing has helped me so much in thinking about this problem as a conversation I had with William Andres, when he was Chairman of Dayton-Hudson Corporation and about to chair a task force on productivity in state government. He asked me, "Is productivity in government something you *do,* or is it something that *happens* if you do the fundamentals right? I'm in retailing," he continued. "In retailing, turnover is very important. Stores that turn over inventory more rapidly are much more profitable. But every time a manager tries to increase turnover, the store isn't profitable anymore. So we decided a long time ago that turnover isn't something you do. We concentrate on getting the fundamentals right."

As Andres was tactfully suggesting, productivity—or innovation of any sort—is something that happens, in both the public and private sectors, when you get the fundamentals right. It has certainly been true in this country's effort to introduce cost control in health care. The efforts to get doctors to "do" cost control were not notably successful. What we're doing instead, as business executives know, is changing the way doctors get paid. In education, too, it will be imperative to deal with the fundamentals.

A System Without Incentives

Education is a service that people are required by law to use, from about age six to age sixteen. It is free in the public schools. Customers can go elsewhere but only at their own expense. The public school system is divided into districts. Within each district there is only one established, or "franchised," public teaching organization, to which the children in that district are assigned. Usually, people can change districts only by moving their place of residence or by paying tuition—again, only at their own expense.

This arrangement—created by the state—clearly was not designed to meet the Peters and Waterman test for excellence: to pay close attention to what customers want, and to innovate constantly[1] The state has given the public education system no real incentive to do that. The combination of mandatory attendance with no tuition ensures that students will come. If the students come, revenue comes, increasingly from the state. And if the revenues are there, the jobs will be there. The system is at risk only for its incremental costs—annual salary increases, capital improvements that require local voter approval, and improvement programs (R&D).

What *is* at risk in this arrangement is performance. Within broad limits, the system provides the schools with what they need, whether or not they make improvements, and independent of how well the children learn. If the schools do try hard to improve—as many do—nothing very good will happen to them. If they fail, nothing very bad will happen to them. The accountability system is fundamentally defective.

For any country serious about excellence in public education, this is an absurd arrangement. I understand and respect what teachers tell me: that it is unfair to lay on them full responsibility for the success of children who are with them only 11 percent of the time between the ages of six and sixteen. But I know at the same time that it is foolish to say that there is no connection at all. Something can be done, and has to be done, to create both negative as well as positive consequences based on the system's performance. This is, Bill Andres' terms, getting the fundamentals right.

Nobody can "make" the educational system change. Like health care, public education is too big and powerful a system to be forced to change, even to accept new technology, if it feels a change is not in its interest. This is why, as so many concerned observers now sense, the conventional reform movement— the "more, longer, harder, tougher" agenda—will probably end in disappointment.

Rewarding Success

It would be better to connect the system's success to the students' success. Altruism is real and important in this system, but something more then simply "feeling better" should be the reward for schools and teachers that do really

[1]Thomas J. Peters and Robert H. Waterman, Jr., *In Search of Excellence*. New York: Harper & Row, 1982.

well for kids. And some kind of adverse consequences need to be created for schools that fail to change and improve.

Of course, there are real problems that come from external sources: the changing demographics of the student population; the new demands imposed by society on the schools; the loss of respect by the public for teachers; and the reluctance of taxpayers to provide adequate, stable and equitable funding.

But the structural problem is also real, and structural change is not on the system's agenda. Rather, the existing arrangement will be taken as a given, and the requests will most likely be for more support, more resources, and even for mandates. We've heard these requests at the Governor's Discussion Group in Minnesota for the past 18 months. Education groups were asking for money for staff development. "Nothing is more important," they said. "If it's that important," the Group asked, "why aren't you doing it now?" There was much clearing of throats and shuffling of papers. "Make it a categorical requirement," they said, "so we *have* to do it."

In a healthy system, an organization has incentives to make improvements on its own. Education should as well. Business efforts to improve education ought to address that fundamental need. But the effort to change what the system takes as "given" will bring business into conflict with the major groups in public education.

Business is reluctant to fight the schools. Business would rather help. I've had community-relations officers tell me, "It's not our job to tell the schools how to run." I've seen public officials confront reformers by saying, "I'm trying to row this boat. Why are you trying to tip it over?" That's tough for an executive or a business firm to deal with. But conflict is inevitable if there is going to be real improvement. It can be done, and it is being done in the business community where I live.

Support from Business

The Minnesota Business Partnership, which includes the CEOs of many of the largest enterprises in the state, put education on its agenda about five years ago, largely at the urging of Lewis Lehr, then Chairman of 3M Company. The group spent more than a quarter-of-a-million dollars to develop an understanding of the system and gave its consultant remarkable encouragement to propose a new plan for organizing schools (not simply a tinkering with the system). The Partnership had the courage to tell Minnesota plainly that "the present system has reached the limits of its effectiveness."

In 1985, when Governor Perpich challenged the Minnesota educational system with his proposal to give students access to public school programs outside their own districts, the Partnership supported him and was vigorously attacked by some powerful educational organizations. But the Partnership continued to insist on the need for choice, the need for assessment, and the need for differentiating the teaching staff. Today, the teachers' union has changed its leadership, and the new president wants to work with the Partnership.

We want to change the "givens" in the system so that it provides districts, schools, and teachers with opportunities to make changes and improvements, and incentives to use those opportunities. Three things can be done.

Three Proposals

First, we should change the relationship between district and school. Research findings show that the school—not the district—should be the unit to focus on for improvement. This confirms what was intuitively obvious: students go to schools, after all, not to districts. We need to delegate more responsibility to the people in the schools to decide how learning can best be organized. Principals, teachers and parents—in some new and more collegial way—need to make the decisions about how time, money, facilities, and people are used. School boards and superintendents will be reluctant to give up their control, but they ought to be setting objectives and monitoring results.

Second, we should change the relationship between teachers and schools. We say that we want to increase the professional autonomy of teachers, yet we do not give teachers the status that defines a professional in most other areas of work. Some professionals can be employees—engineers, architects, journalists, doctors and lawyers. But many work for themselves, and all have the opportunity to do so if they wish. No such choice is available to a teacher. If you want to be a teacher, you have to be an employee.

We ought to give teachers the option to work for themselves. We might let a group of math teachers, for example, form a small professional practice. They would decide on their own approach to learning, perhaps a problem-solving approach. The teachers would select their own colleagues, pick their own materials, and decide who would teach what and when. They would be paid a lump sum to cover salaries, fringe benefits and other costs. They would decide among themselves how to share the money. If they were successful, they might begin to work for more than a single school. Their professional responsibility and income could then grow.

I have asked math teachers what they would do differently were such an arrangement in effect. Quickly they converted the question: What can we do to improve student learning that would not require us to spend money we could otherwise keep? And they answer that they would expand peer teaching and self-directed study, involve parents and others in the community more often, differentiate staff, and introduce new learning technology.

Third, we need to change the relationship between the system and its users. Within public education, we need to shift the mechanism by which a student gets to a school from assignment to choice. If we do this we can let decisions about improvement remain local, which is an important part of our public school tradition. We would not need mandates, which only enforce minimum requirements. We can even let districts decide not to improve, because no district will be able to do so without consequences. Districts and schools do not want to lose

22

students. If there is a risk that the kids will leave, the schools will respond with improvements.

Educational groups will resist this, even if the movement of students is controlled for equity and confined within the public system. The argument will not be that it is bad for administrators, but that it will be bad for students and for the public. But choice for students, unsettling as it will be for schools, is one of the fundamentals that we have to get right. People in business understand opportunities and incentives. Education, like other systems, behaves the way it is structured and rewarded to behave. If we reward success, we may get success. The students should not have to be the ones at risk.

Business-Education Initiatives: An Assessment

Marsha Levine
Associate Director
Educational Issues Department
American Federation of Teachers

Some time has passed since the first business-education initiatives were taken, and this is a good time to review the expectations, the investments, the results, and the changes.

In looking back over the terrain, I observe three primary shifts. First, the focus has shifted from a narrow set of curricular goals to a concern for broader liberal education. Second, there has been a shift from local-level partnerships to state- and national-level partnerships. Third, there is now more involvement in policy-making.

Initial Steps

In 1980, I was a policy fellow in the U.S. Department of Education. It was my assignment to be the departmental liaison to interest groups and outside constituencies in the educational process. While the range of groups that formed the constituency of the public schools seemed overwhelming, one group was notable by its absence—the business community.

At the same time, newspapers, magazines and journals were featuring articles about productivity problems in the United States and about the need to be competitive in an international economy. People began talking about the relationship between a strong economy and a good educational system, about the stake the business community had in the public schools, and about something called "human capital development."

A variety of school and business collaborations appeared on the horizon: adopt-a-school programs; business volunteers working in the schools; donations from businesses, ranging from surplus furniture to computer systems. Business and education people in local communities started seeking out ways to talk to one another. Linking organizations sprang up all over, including public education funds and business-education task forces sponsored by local Chambers of Commerce.

Most programs were school assistance efforts, and we began to have great expectations for their success. Some believed that the private sector might fill in the gaps created by cutbacks in government spending. However, others feared that such involvement would reduce the pressure for public support of public schools. Educators, who had already lost support as a result of declines in the public school population, saw the business community as a potentially powerful ally—but one whose involvement might result in distorted goals or "vocationalization." Education for the common good might lose out to education for personal or corporate gain.

Still, the alliance was attractive and became even more so as business recognized its need for a well-educated, not a narrowly trained, citizenry. Employers would have the opportunity to tell educators what young people need to learn in order to be employable. Another powerful motive was that business could use its influence to mobilize support for public schools. The publication of *A Nation At Risk* provided further impetus, including participation from the national business community.[1]

Changing Relationships

How did the nature of private-sector involvement change? Hundreds of partnerships developed between schools and corporations—big, multinational corporations as well as small businesses. Some partnerships focused on funding—like the Boston Plan for Excellence, an endowment established by Boston corporations for the benefit of the city's schools. Others were aimed at teachers, such as Philadelphia's Program for the Advancement of the Teaching of the Humanities (PATHS), which provides staff development, recognition and rewards for public school teachers. Still others targeted students—like Jobs for America's Graduates, a national school-to-work transition program designed to improve the skills of "at-risk" students. Some partnerships focused on the transfer of management expertise from corporate executives to school executives—like the D.C. Management Institute.

In addition, some businesses entered the state policy arena through coalitions. Hundreds of business-education task forces were created. Major educational initiatives were undertaken by Business Round Tables in California, Minnesota and Washington.

A survey that the Committee for Economic Development conducted in 1984, and updated in 1986, found that among smaller firms, only 19 percent of respondents indicated involvement. In contrast, over half of the large businesses participated in some business-education collaboration.[2] The extent of financial support

---

[1] *A Nation at Risk,* report of the National Commission on Excellence in Education, 1983.

[2] Marsha Levine, "Survey of Employer Needs," Committee for Economic Development, New York, 1985.

is less impressive. Recent data from the Council for Financial Aid to Education indicated a total of $1.7 billion given to education, 5.2 percent of which is directed at elementary and secondary education. That comes to roughly $2 per child.

What *are* the results of business-education partnerships and how can we measure them? It seems to me that the efforts begun in the early 1980s were instrumental in bringing business and public education together and each learned about the other's needs and ways of doing things. The benefits may extend well beyond the business-education partnerships themselves. It is clear that business has become serious about its stake in quality public schools, and the educational community has put its most central public policy issues on the agenda for discussion with business. The risk level has gone up but so has the possibility for real change in the public schools.

Business has played a role in helping to establish the reform agenda; furthermore, its perspectives have an influence on the way that agenda is being addressed. These then are the questions: What is on the agenda? And what has business to offer on those issues?

The Second Phase

Many of my colleagues have observed that we are now, in fact, into the second phase of educational reform. The first focused on making the present system work better. Improvements were to come through *more*—more time, more courses, more requirements, more rigorous standards. These reforms were undoubtedly needed in many places where the system had become lax and standards had declined. But "necessary" changes are not always sufficient. The second wave came as it became clear that a different approach was needed to meet the challenges in public education. One fundamental challenge had to be met: to educate *all* children as well as we educate the elite few.

We will not achieve this goal simply by making the present system more demanding, raising standards for students, lengthening school years, increasing requirements, and offering merit pay to teachers. A persistently high dropout rate (as high as 40 percent in some of our urban districts) will not be reduced by demanding more of students who are already disengaged. Poor performance on tests that measure thinking skills, problem-solving, writing skills, and reading comprehension will not be affected by doing "more of the same." Traditional ways of dealing with teacher shortages would only fill classrooms with individuals who are neither suited nor qualified for the demanding practice of teaching.

All of this adds up not only to doing things better, but also to doing them differently, and thus the second wave of reform deals with change. The business community has played an important role in helping us to understand that concept. In particular, two national efforts that have been instrumental in identifying and articulating these key ideas are the Committee for Economic Development and the Carnegie Forum on Education and the Economy—both combine the talent and leadership of the educational community and the business sector.

Four Key Issues

It has become clear that improving the quality of education hinges upon being able to attract and retain education's share of the best and the brightest. This is difficult, however, because of the structure of the teaching profession and of the ways in which schools are organized and managed—ways that undermine professional practice. Dealing with such issues is central to the second stage of reform, which must focus on *restructuring, accountability, choice,* and *distribution of resources.*

Business has contributed a great deal to our understanding of how best to structure an organization. The experiences of teaching, learning, and doing business all support increased control at the school and classroom level, where the work of the organization is actually done. A "restructured" school relies on teachers' expertise in designing and implementing learning environments. It recognizes the importance of people working together by providing time for teachers to talk shop, learn from one another, get feedback, and address the problems they share. These are characteristics of smart work places—and we have learned a lot about them from business.

The second issue is accountability—increased teaching responsibility requires higher standards for teachers. The public must be confident that teachers are prepared to accept and execute that responsibility and teachers must be assured that there will be sufficient, appropriate resources and training available to prepare them to meet that challenge.

Equally important is employee participation and involvement. The people closest to the actual production—the teacher in a school, the employee in a business—must be relied upon. There's a better chance of a quality outcome when employees are involved in setting standards and in defining and solving problems. And when there is flexibility in how they work, they can more readily maintain those standards.

A third issue, choice, involves giving consumers a say in where they send their children to school. Theoretically, at least, favored schools would become the competition and would provide an incentive for other schools to improve.

Matching students' interests and capabilities with program offerings can result in students working harder. Having a choice can stimulate interest and effort; this holds for students as well as for teachers. I agree with those who view choice in the public sector as a way of increasing options for parents, students and teachers—whose choices may now be limited by inadequate resources or inflexible school administration. But I would caution against the pitfalls involved, such as segregation by race, class or ability. Such an outcome would be antithetical to the mission of public schools in our society. On the whole, the business community appears to support that mission and the role that public education plays in fostering democratic values—which is what allows business to thrive.

The final item deals with the distribution of resources. How should the funds that we have be spent? Once again the business perspective is consistent with research findings and supported by good practice. That perspective recognizes education as an investment in human capital and not as a social-service expenditure. The experience of business also suggests looking for investment prospects with high rates of return. The Committee for Economic Development reports that return on investment in the education of young children at risk is as high as four to one—in terms of money not spent later on remedial education, unemployment, welfare, health care, and crime prevention.[3]

Each of these areas—restructuring, accountability, choice and distribution of resources—is complex, and the involvement of the business community adds a new level of complexity. One of the by-products of maturing business-education relationships has been a deepening concern about the connection between economic growth and public education. That concern has manifested itself in an engagement of the public and the private sectors on some basic educational policy issues. Teachers in classrooms talk about "teachable moments"—those times when the *need* to know and the *opportunity* to learn come together. Perhaps this is such a moment for American education. At the very least, there is a climate of mutual engagement and a focus on change.

[3]Report of Select Committee on Children, Youth and Families, U.S. House of Representatives, Washington, D.C., 1985.

Matching Needs and Resources

Patrick Manders
Publisher, ProEducation Magazine

How can we work actively to promote business-education partnerships? People have been discussing ideas, recommendations and resources for years, but now it's time to act. What ProEducation Magazine is doing is called the "ProEducation National Initiative: Matching Schools' Needs With Business Resources." It's an initiative, not a research project, designed to promote action in partnerships and has been a major project of ours for more than a year.

The first step is to take a survey of the educational needs in this country by asking teachers about problems they deal with in the classroom (see Exhibit). This will be followed by a survey of business resources available on a national level for educational programs. Finally, the needs will be matched with the resources in a partnership-opportunities list—a list of projects that use known business resources to address known educational needs.

We launched the project by touring the country to get representative geographic and demographic input from teachers about universal problems in the classroom. The sites we chose had to have successful partnership programs already in place. The five-day tour included St. Petersburg, St. Louis, Los Angeles, Seattle, and New York City.

Each meeting lasted a full day, and included two teachers from each of seven disciplines—mathematics, science, English, social studies, distributive education, home economics, and career guidance—plus partnership coordinators. The participating teachers at each site were selected from the entire school district, with the help of the coordinators, and were chosen based on their excellence and their interest in improving their schools.

These focus groups met without any administrators in the room, to encourage truly open response. We asked for a discussion of all problems, regardless of whether the teachers thought businesses could help. As questions arose in certain topic areas, each teacher had the chance to speak individually before any general discussion began.

These are the topics we covered, with some of the more common responses from the focus groups:

1. *What are the teachers' perceptions of business in general?*

Many teachers felt that concern from the business sector is often superficial, aimed at improving corporate public relations or image. They felt that businesses were often condescending in talking about education. Teachers were skeptical of partnership programs that didn't ask for their suggestions. Although they expressed caution, they consider business in general to be a good potential resource. In each city, teachers with experience in partnerships with business reported positive results.

2. *What are the students' perceptions of business in general?*

It was the teachers' opinion that students at the secondary-school level don't understand the real world of work; they have glamorous views of business and are interested in making money rather than following specific career paths. But teachers said also that students who had been involved in partnerships and exposed to business had come away with positive reactions. Exposure to the business world had broken down the barriers.

3. *What are the teachers' perceptions of the business-education partnership concept?*

The teachers saw partnership with business as a relationship involving mutual goals, understanding, trust and respect; as a union between equals relying on open dialogue, ongoing commitment, shared responsibility, and shared resources; and as a joint venture aimed at improving the same product: students. The only concern repeatedly mentioned was over the *process* of the programs—who would be involved? what would be the objectives? The concept of partnership itself was never questioned.

4. *What problems and needs do teachers see in the classroom?*

We took a vote after each session to determine the top five problems. The following list represents the consensus of all the focus groups:

> (1) *Student problems*—poor attendance, motivation, and attitude; high level of dropout; drug abuse; after-school jobs that hurt academic performance.
> (2) *Teacher morale*—teacher shortages, large workload and class size, stress, poor self-esteem.
> (3) *Budgetary problems*—lack of funds for buildings, equipment, and other facilities.
> (4) *Faulty curriculum*—irrelevance to the working world, lack of long-term career considerations.
> (5) *Administrative problems*—lack of management ability in administration, poor work distribution, seniority system of promotion, unrealistic demands on teachers.

32

Here's Your School's Chance to be Heard!

Please have a representative from your school complete and return this anonymous questionnaire. Your school's input will be included in a presentation to national business leaders at our ProEducation National Initiative Business/Education Focus Group, where partnership programs and solutions will be formulated.

Please respond to the following questions by checking the appropriate box (es).

1 Your title/position:

□ principal
□ teacher
□ department head
□ counselor
□ other

2 School size:

□ less than 300 students
□ 300-800 students
□ over 800 students

3 School type:

□ elementary
□ middle/junior
□ high school
□ college/university

4 School location:

□ urban
□ suburban
□ rural/small town

5 State (postal abbreviation):

_____

6 What is your school's general perception of business?

□ very positive
□ somewhat positive
□ neutral
□ somewhat negative
□ very negative

7 Is your school currently involved in any business/education partnerships?

□ yes
□ no

8 If not, do you feel your school would be interested in establishing such partnerships in the future?

□ yes
□ no

9 Briefly, what do you see as the biggest potential drawback to business/education partnerships?

_____
_____

10 What role(s) do you feel business/ education partnerships should play?

Curriculum-based:

□ provide elements of the basic curriculum
□ supplement the basic curriculum
□ provide updates to curriculum regarding new technologies, trends, etc.

Student-based:

□ develop programs to contribute to student growth
□ provide role models for students
□ provide hands-on exposure to business
□ nurture students' general awareness of business world
□ nurture students' basic social skills
□ develop programs to help problem students
□ illuminate career paths for students

Teacher-based:

□ give teachers organizational support
□ provide teaching modules relative to business world
□ give teachers meaningful summer employment
□ fill out teacher experience with business exposure

Based on provision of resources:

□ provide business personnel to play a classroom role
□ provide access to business expertise in all areas
□ provide access to business facilities and equipment
□ provide financial support to the schools
□ provide materials or in-kind contributions
□ provide organizational/management advice
□ act as protagonist for the schools, lobbying on school's behalf, etc.

Based on the business/education relationship itself:

□ make business more aware of the human realities of the school
□ open channels of communication between school and business community
□ make schools more aware of the needs of business (which students will be expected to meet)
□ explore and pursue mutual goals
□ provide mutual exposure/awareness to all involved

11 What type(s) of support do you feel are most needed from business?

Would they be programs to address...

□ student motivation
□ development of students' basic values
□ teacher morale
□ teacher efficacy in communication process
□ teacher training
□ teachers' professional development and career path development
□ teacher shortage
□ teacher recognition
□ teacher workload
□ budgeting
□ teacher salary
□ equipment shortages
□ school facilities
□ resource planning
□ administration/management problems
□ school system bureaucracy
□ community involvement in school affairs
□ school and teacher image problems
□ overcrowding
□ school system structure
□ bilingual education
□ relevance of curriculum to business/ society
□ remedial teaching
□ curriculum content
□ security/safety in the schools
□ graduate job availability
□ delineating family/school responsibilities
□ illiteracy
□ inadequate parental involvement
□ inequity of student abilities
□ social pressures on students
□ family & society problems
□ racial considerations
□ desegregation
□ dealing with multiple cultures
□ other

THANK YOU!

Please remove this survey, fold and return it to us today. Your input will be counted.

Other problems included racism, bureaucracy, security, vandalism and salary.

From these focus group discussions, we developed survey questionnaires which we sent out in ProEducation Magazine to a targeted mailing (see Exhibit). The responses we received were surprising. Ninety percent of the schools listed a positive or very positive attitude toward business. About 70 percent were currently involved in partnership programs, and of the remainder, more than 90 percent said they would be interested.

Successful business-education partnerships usually have certain elements in common, and we use the word RAPPORT to stand for the seven necessary components:

- *Reason:* The reason for each partner's involvement must be sincere and realistic, or the superficiality will become apparent and the partnership will degenerate into "take what you can get."
- *Attitude:* An attitude of cooperation and mutual respect must underlie the partnership, and business must avoid the condescending role of an "expert" coming to correct inadequacies with limited involvement.
- *Person:* The selection of the individuals involved must be based on their sincere commitment to the partnership effort as well as their qualifications and ability to get the job done.
- *Period:* Meaningful programs require commitment and continuity over a long period if students and teachers are to place any faith in them.
- *Organization:* Following up on the logical steps in any project—from researching to budgeting, planning, launching, and guiding the project—is crucial to the success of the program. It helps ensure that the partners' goals are not in conflict.
- *Relationship:* The partners must be equals, so that each will feel that he or she is contributing and that the attributes of each will be recognized and used.
- *Teacher input:* Teacher input and support is essential to the formulation of programs designed for the classroom.

Our next step is to assemble a National Business Focus Group in New York City. Selected top executives from business and industry will be asked to match current and potential resources to specific needs. If the necessary resources don't exist, then the group will be asked to explore creative alternatives to solving the problems at hand.

The Partnership Opportunities List that we will develop as a result of our focus group meetings will be actively promoted to the business community at large in hopes that business will sponsor various programs on the list—all of which will be targeted toward addressing established educational problems in a systematic, nationally coordinated fashion.

Partnerships—Three Examples

Tenneco Adopts a School

[Two Tenneco executives—Jo Ann Swinney, *Director of Community Affairs,* and Gordon B. Bonfield, *Senior Vice President and Group Executive*—briefly described a successful local program.]

Tenneco has a business-school partnership program that began as a result of something our head of long-range planning said: "The corporation should act as a good citizen." In response to this, we designed an investment program for secondary education.

I contacted the school district to identify the school with the worst problems. We recruited our employees to help teachers in that school by serving as special speakers, tutors, classroom teachers or assistants. Next, we brought together teachers and company volunteers to develop common goals.

After two years, we recognized that the difficulties were much more extensive than we had expected and not limited to academic problems. So we brought an outside organization to our adopted school to determine more specifically what problems were holding back students.

Students who were most likely to drop out were our primary concern. We instituted a job program to encourage students to stay in school. Other incentives included awards for perfect monthly and yearly attendance. Simultaneously, we began to recruit summer employment sponsors from educational institutions, social-service organizations, and city government. We informed these potential employers that participating students would not be "average" students, but rather students at risk. Sponsors were asked to serve as mentors and to shepherd students through the program.

We also developed a leadership program with the Tomorrow's America Foundation. We took a portion of the Foundation's curriculum, added items that we wanted, and got the approval of the school board. In this program, the students go through an intensive four-day program to develop leadership qualities, communication skills, problem-solving abilities, and self-esteem. Student response has been surprisingly positive; teacher and student morale went up 100 percent, according to the school's principal.

Saturday Academy

[Badi G. Foster, *President, AEtna Institute for Corporate Education,* outlined an initiative that supplements and supports the local school system.]

AEtna operates a Saturday Academy in Hartford, Connecticut for inner-city children in middle schools, using teachers from the public schools. The child brings along a parent (or other significant adult) to the Academy on Saturdays; there are parental programs as well as activities for the adult and the child to take part in together.

Three main factors contribute to the success of the program: (1) eighteen months of planning with community-based organizations, the school system, and the company; (2) the positive attitude and the competence of the staff; and (3) the pleasant environment. The seventh-graders were treated as adults, and at no point did we have problems of poor behavior or vandalism.

The Academy is also successful because of the "joint ownership" among the community, the school, and AEtna. In negotiating the creation of the program, we forged new links among these three groups.

The heavy stress on parent (or adult) participation strengthens the relationships of teachers, students, and parents. The mix of participants has helped to create a network of parents and children that crosses racial, ethnic, and neighborhood lines.

The selection of public-school teachers to work in the Academy emphasizes their value as effective teachers in the public schools. And the enrichment curriculum is designed to enhance the curriculum of the public school, not to replace or counteract it.

Investment Gone Awry: Case Study and Lessons

[Edward A. Fox, *President and Chief Executive Officer, Student Loan Marketing Association,* explained how good intentions—along with money—can evaporate and how that result can be avoided.]

Business has been investing in education—or at least making contributions to education—for some time. What I see now is a more disciplined approach to those contributions. In this era of managing for results, companies are beginning to contribute for results—educational results, rather than public-relations gains. This means that business will be putting more into the relationship than just money—though the money remains important—and that educators will be held accountable for more than just good ideas.

This new kind of business-education relationship relies on definite objectives, useful assessment procedures, commitment to follow through, and people—in partnerships far more structured than those in the past.

Specifically, these relationships must be based on clearly defined, understood and measurable objectives. Whether the undertaking is a one-time project in support of the local high school or a multi-year initiative with national implications, all parties to the partnership should subscribe to the same goals and define individual targets at the outset. Business should never invest for itself and for its shareholders without defined objectives; it should not be willing to do so when it invests for the sake of education.

The method of measuring a project's success, both incrementally and ultimately, must be agreed upon from the start and applied objectively at agreed-upon points along the way. Only in this way will all eyes remain focused on original goals or will necessary adjustments be recognized and made. Again, this is standard operating procedure for business when it enters into any venture.

Other critical ingredients are the involvement of the company's employees and a real commitment from its top management. It simply doesn't work to put up the bucks alone. Money—although it may speak—does not manage. Nor is real progress measured in dollars spent, per project or per student. Only people—and their hands-on involvement—can assure that dollars are well spent.

Finally, productive investment in education, like sound investment in anything else, requires continuity and consistency—staying power. That does not mean continuing down the wrong path if periodic measurements indicate a shift is in order. It does mean committing to provide the resources, both financial and human, over a sufficient period to achieve the objectives set forth at the outset.

This list of prerequisites doesn't come from a textbook; I put it together myself—based on 20-20 hindsight.

A couple of years ago, in keeping with our commitment to education and to our community in Washington, D.C., the Student Loan Marketing Association gave a significant amount of money to help launch what was envisioned as a major partnership effort involving a private foundation, local business, and the local school system. The goal was a laudable one: reducing unemployment among city youths. The money that we and the foundation provided was intended to "leverage" other business contributions—both in funds and service.

We were to provide on-site training for the teachers so that, in developing curriculum, they would become more aware of the job opportunities to which their students could aspire. As another component, our business managers were to share their planning expertise with school-system administrators. The whole package was coordinated by a local community foundation. We were excited and so were others. The project papers were rather impressive. Press releases went out—locally as well as nationally. We thought this undertaking would be replicated in other communities. Even the project papers documenting the results sounded pretty good.

In all candor, however, an estimated quarter-of-a-million dollars in funds and nearly a million dollars of in-kind services produced little more than those project papers. We started with a very good idea but had not clearly defined specific objectives, periodic measurement of progress, and individual responsibilities. After the public-relations flurry, the effort became fragmented to the extent that it had any reality at all.

I do not like to publicize failures any more than anyone else does. Nor do I wish to point fingers, especially since one would be directed at us. Rather, in relating this experience, I hope to help others avoid similar failures and to point out some of the lessons we learned.

In particular, we feel that two types of effort will make business investment in education more meaningful for both partners. First, there is an opportunity to research what others have done—what has worked and what has not, and why. Second, many who want to support productive partnerships with education would welcome the development of a results-oriented approach to partnership.

A New Education Agenda for Business
Workshop Sessions

Leonard Lund
Senior Research Associate and Conference Project Director
The Conference Board, Inc.

Overview

In addition to providing an opportunity for participants to exchange experiences and information, four concurrent workshops at the conference were designed to generate new ideas on how business might take the next steps in the educational reform movement. The workshops addressed major issues—demographic trends, employment patterns, local involvement, and policy development—from the point of view of how business should focus its efforts.

While each workshop began with an examination of a specific aspect of business-education relations, the general discussions revolved around two central issues: how to strengthen ongoing business-education collaborations and how to make the contribution of business to educational reform most effective. Significantly, there never was any doubt expressed that business was not intent upon continuing its involvement and expanding its role in education.

The creation of a line of communication between business people and educators in the common cause of school reform was identified as a major accomplishment of school-business parterships to date. Nonetheless, one of the principal recommendations of the workshops addressed problems in communications. Evidently there are still areas of misunderstanding, particularly with respect to the jargon of the different cultures. There is a need to devise common definitions, so that, for example, school measurements may be equated with those of the workplace—what *does* an eighth-grade reading level mean to an employer?

Another key area of concern relates to the transition from school to work and work-readiness. Participants noted a gap between curriculum planning in the schools and the needs of job developers in industry. The result is a continuing mismatch between the schools and the workplace. Though there were few references to vocational education, there was a call for transition programs that emphasize training in workplace behavior and pre-graduation work experience. Recommendations also included counseling in elementary and middle schools to discourage dropping out and to introduce career options.

Expanding business involvement, conferees agreed, means not only attracting more businesses to education partnerships, but also creating broader community coalitions. System-wide collaborations can better deal with a wide range of community problems that affect learning and provide opportunities for smaller businesses with fewer resources to play a role.

The most innovative and far-reaching recommendations dealt with internal corporate perceptions, structures and programs. Most notable is the proposal for the CEO's active involvement in the creation and development of corporate policy toward education. This would, many said, ensure consistency in a company approach to public schools in all locations, in the actions of all company officers and departments, and in the support of public policy. Any criticism of business was largely directed at its timidity in stating its expectations and in demanding better results from the schools.

Company policy, it was suggested, should also include financial contributions to elementary and secondary schools. Here the hope is that corporate contributions for education will be perceived not as charity but as investments in the future workforce and as part of human resources or employee training budgets. Furthermore, these investments should be accompanied by an appraisal using some concrete measurements of outcome that are meaningful and acceptable to both educators and employers.

Damning Demographics

This workshop explored the complex relationships among demographic trends, education and the economy. Anthony Carnevale, Chief Economist and Vice President, American Society for Training and Development, opened the session with some observations about the economic benefits of education—which is itself a big business. The nation's educational system is a $250-billion-a-year enterprise, funded mostly by public spending. In addition, companies spend about $30 billion each year in formal training of employees and about $180 billion for informal training or "on-the-job coaching."

That money is not going to waste. Education's contribution to overall growth in national income, statistics show, has exceeded that of machine capital since 1929. Even in the years 1973-81, when productivity growth declined, education still contributed substantially to the gross national product (GNP)—accounting for one-third of total GNP growth.

Extending this analysis suggests that today's educational system is laying the basis of tomorrow's economy. It communicates knowledge, molds the work force, and contributes to the growth and spread of technology—all of which is economic "seed corn." In the long term, education has a powerful, proactive relationship to the economy. In the short term, however, the economy dictates the type and level of education that society needs to fill the available jobs.

Up to now, Carnevale said, the major achievement of the U.S. educational system has been the growth in the percentage of the population that has graduated from high school. Demographic trends indicate that in the future, the system will have to be geared to produce graduates of a higher caliber. Opportunities for economic growth once stemmed in part from the sheer increase in number of those entering the work force, but in the future there will be a smaller cohort of young people. The future task of education is thus not simply to reduce the number of drop outs, but also to prepare young people for the higher demands of an evolving economy.

Education also has a profound impact on the community and the individual. Carnevale noted that $3,000 for one year of preschool education for a disadvantaged child can save the community as much as $20,000 a year in welfare, unemployment, or crime-related costs. After a child reaches age 20, that one year of early education seems to continue producing benefits, including better earning potential. For the U.S. population as a whole, a high school education is worth an extra $109,000 in lifetime earnings; a college education creates an extra $226,000 in earnings.

There are economic benefits for the employer, too. Education has been found to correlate strongly with the work ethic: The higher the educational achievement, the greater the employee's commitment to the job. A job's level and complexity correlate with the degree of preparation acquired in school: Among professionals, managers and technical workers, 66 percent reported that they learned all or most of what they needed to know for their first job in school. In contrast, service and craft workers reported that they learned more of what they needed to know in the workplace. One of the implications of this finding is that schools will play an increasingly important role as jobs become more complex.

Looking to the future, Carnevale noted the following demographic trends:

- The 16- to 24-age cohort is supplying fewer entrants to the labor market, which may create a "mismatch"—too few people and too many jobs.
- The people who will comprise that age group will be those in whom "investment" by family and school has traditionally been insufficient—minorities, females, the handicapped, and the disadvantaged.

This means that the future work force cannot measure up to the current one either in quality or quantity. And there will be greater competition for these young people from higher education, the military, and the public sector.

How are these emerging realities in the workplace being addressed? Carnevale noted that current trends in business and in educational reform are both heading in the same direction. Business restructuring is decentralizing facilities, which will eventually mean that employees at the points of production and sales will have greater responsibilities and control over more resources. A similar movement is evident in the proposals for educational reform. Greater autonomy will be vested in the individual school and even in the classroom, the point of production in education. This shift will require new ways of measuring outcome and new accountability for education. The public sector as a whole, however, is not accustomed to—or organized for—measuring success by outcome and will find it difficult to make this transition.

Finally, Carnevale observed that the relationship between business and education is based on accountability and measured outcomes. This works both ways: Educators need to be accountable for their product and business people need to communicate more effectively what they are looking for and what they need. Ultimately, the goal is enough jobs and the right kinds of education so that business can guarantee young people a job based on their educational performance.

Carnevale concluded with this comment:

> We have the makings of a solution here that is optimistic from the educators' and the students' perspective, if somewhat troublesome from the business community's perspective. I think the incentive for business is to be more accountable to education in the sense of trying to reward people for doing well in school and trying to choose employees on the basis of some accountable measure of their performance in school.

The workshop discussion, led by consultant Rita Kaplan, formerly Manager of Education Programs for Honeywell in Minneapolis, centered around the issue of how to measure outcome and accountability. Many participants—representing both business and academia—saw a need for a better level of communication between business and schools. In part this entails creating better definitions of job skills or requirements that both business executives and educators can rely on. Business leaders should contribute their ideas and expertise in the making of educational policies, especially the hard decisions on resource allocation and identification of the key economic needs in the community. Others noted that business could provide more realistic views of the world for young people.

Based on the participants' remarks, Rita Kaplan identified a number of items for the "new agenda":

- Education needs input from business executives who specialize in training and human resources. These experts offer experience and insight into the issues of evaluating performance.
- Business must get involved in creating role models for students who are unfamiliar with employment opportunities.
- Through better communication, executives can contribute to the development of a common approach to such issues as restructuring enterprises and organizational development.
- Business has to be more willing to share the expertise, influence and authority of its top executives in order to help formulate and execute educational policy for the community.

Business + Education = Employment

This session began with a presentation on how changing job requirements are affecting educational reform. The speaker, Sue Berryman, is the Director of the National Center on Education and Employment at Columbia University.

Under the influences of international competition, deregulation, and new technologies, U.S. industries are changing and restructuring corporate organization and work patterns. By doing so, they are altering existing job functions and skill requirements. Research by the Center on Education and Employment has uncovered profound changes in the skills required in the insurance and banking fields, for example. Similar studies will be conducted for business services, the garment trades, and electronics manufacturing.

Many people assumed that computers would simply lower the skills needed for most routine clerical activities in insurance companies. But the study found that computer technology has instead forced the combination of simple jobs into one fairly complex function that requires a higher level of skills. For example, where insurance companies used to hire high school graduates for each of these five jobs, they now hire individuals with at least two years of college for the restructured job of claims adjuster.

The banking industry has undergone comparable change in jobs and skill requirements. While a bank teller's work has become more simple and routine, that of clerk/typist has become more complex. Once restricted to filling out loan and credit card applications, the clerk/typist today is also responsible for handling and understanding a wide array of financial instruments. Bank officers, once primarily marketers, must also be specialists now—as financial or computer-systems analysts, for example.

Skill changes now pervasive in the service industries will spread to the manufacturing sector, where computer-allied production processes are becoming more common. These requirements will have to be considered in educational reform efforts, so that the skills that are taught—verbal, mathematical, conceptual, problem-solving—match the direction of skill changes demanded in the economy.

We are currently ill-equipped to meet this challenge, Berryman contends. The economy needs and rewards a wide array of skills, not narrowly defined verbal and mathematical abilities. As she puts it:

- Social scientists explain and predict individual educational achievement quite successfully, but we do a fairly rotten job of predicting occupational attainment, whether measured by occupational status or wages. Educational achievement does *not* predict occupational attainment all that well. Skills other than those we measure and reward in school are important in determining success in the labor market.
- We see surprising variations in educational attainment among those working—even in high-status, white-collar jobs. Look at the education of those classified in the 1980 U.S. Census as working in management. Fifty percent of the nation's chief executives in 1980 had no more than a high school degree.

Nor can reforms be imposed across the board on all students in the same way, Berryman asserts. The drive to match academic requirements to higher skill levels may not be applied realistically to the growing numbers of students from the ranks of at-risk children, many of whom may not be prepared to perform jobs requiring more skills. In essence, there is a need to take a broader view of educational reform, one that provides alternatives for children at risk, children with advantages, and adults in retraining programs. This approach would permit students to make choices relating to their perceptions of their needs, desires and talents, and not be limited by the core curriculum of the high school.

For some children, vocational education—even programs riddled with serious structural problems—may have value. A study of high school students in the vocational track found that the vocational group focused closely on the workplace, that the vocational track fit their objectives, and that they developed positive attitudes toward school.

In the workshop discussion, led by Renee Berger, President of Teamworks, participants expressed concern about broadening school experience and employment opportunities. For example, for many jobs in the service sector now, a restructured high school curriculum could produce graduates with the skills needed for jobs we now fill with college graduates. Some discussants said that any student could be trained for employment, given good grounding in reading, writing and mathematics and in the basics of appropriate behavior for the workplace. Schools also need to develop entrepreneurial talent, since one out of seven high school graduates opens a business.

Significant attention was directed to ways to prepare high school students for success in the workplace. Several people recounted their experiences with "co-op" education programs, in which students spend a portion of the school year in part-time jobs. Some participants noted that there are not enough quality job sites for co-op programs and that more business involvement is needed. Moreover, there are available jobs in fields that are not attractive to young people, such as air conditioning and refrigeration. Part of the problem is a lack of career counseling.

Reviewing the comments of the workshop participants, Berger concluded that they supported efforts to orient students toward the workplace, for business to share management capabilities with the schools, and for business to assist students in the lower grades (particularly in the ninth and tenth grades) with career choices.

The participants encouraged better communications between business executives and educators. What, for example, do educators mean by an "eighth-grade reading level" and how does it relate to the ability to function in the work force? In turn, business people could clarify for educators the kinds of training workers need to fill present and future jobs.

Local Efforts: The Here and Now

Led by Gordon Bonfield and Jo Ann Swinney of Tenneco, Inc., this group examined the role of business in individual communities. In her opening comments, Swinney noted that much business involvement in schools loses impact because of a lack of common ground. Business finds itself approaching the educational community and saying, "We want to help but we don't know how."